Sustainability Matters:

Navigating the Path to a Greener Future"

S.F OLA

ACKNOWLEDGMENTS

The creation of this book would not have been possible without the support and guidance of many individuals. First and foremost, I would like to express my gratitude to my family and friends, who have provided me with endless encouragement and inspiration throughout this journey. I would like to extend my sincere thanks to the experts and organizations in the field of environmental sustainability, whose work has informed and enriched this book. Your dedication to this cause is truly inspiring, and I am grateful for the opportunity to learn from you. Finally, I would like to thank the readers of this book for taking an interest in environmental sustainability and for your commitment to making a difference. Your actions, no matter how small, have the power to create positive change, and I hope that this book will inspire you to take action.

Introduction:

This book provides a comprehensive overview of environmental sustainability, including its definition, importance, and the challenges and opportunities related to promoting sustainability. The book is structured in a way that makes it accessible to a wide range of readers, from students and environmental advocates to policymakers and business leaders.

The book starts with an introduction that provides a definition of environmental sustainability and explores its importance. The next section of the book focuses on the natural environment and the ecosystems that support life on earth, including the importance of biodiversity, climate change, and the impacts of air and water pollution.

The book then examines the human impact on the environment and the challenges associated with overconsumption and unsustainable practices. Topics covered in this section include deforestation, overfishing, soil degradation, and plastic pollution.

The book then focuses on solutions for environmental sustainability, including renewable energy, sustainable agriculture, conservation and protection of biodiversity, and the importance of reducing, reusing, and recycling. The section on government and business action for sustainability explores the role of regulations, corporate social responsibility, public-private partnerships, and the role of consumers in driving change.

The final section of the book looks to the future of environmental sustainability and the emerging technologies and innovations that can help us achieve a more sustainable future. The section also explores the importance of global cooperation and education and awareness in promoting environmental sustainability.

In conclusion, this book provides a comprehensive overview of environmental sustainability and the actions necessary to promote sustainability. Through its accessible and engaging style, the book aims to inspire readers to take action in their own lives to help create a more sustainable future.

I: ENVIRONMENTAL SUSTAINABILITY OVERVIEW

Definition of Environmental Sustainability:

Environmental sustainability is a critical issue facing the world today, as human activities continue to have a profound impact on the natural environment. From climate change and air pollution to water pollution and soil degradation, the health of our planet is at risk. The importance of environmental sustainability cannot be overstated, as it affects not only the natural world but also the well-being of all-natural environment and its ecosystems, the human impact on the environment, and the solutions and actions necessary to promote sustainability. The goal of this book is to provide a comprehensive overview of the challenges and opportunities related to environmental sustainability and to inspire readers to take action in their own lives to promote a sustainable future.

Environmental sustainability refers to the responsible use and management of natural resources so that they are available for future generations. It involves meeting the needs of the present without compromising the ability of future generations to meet their own needs. This means that we must use resources in a manner that does not cause long-term harm to the environment and ensures the health and well-being of both current and future generations.

Environmental sustainability is about balancing the economic, social, and environmental needs of society in a responsible and equitable way. It involves considering the impacts of our actions on the natural world and making choices that promote the long-term health and stability of the planet. This includes reducing greenhouse gas emissions, preserving biodiversity, protecting sensitive ecosystems, and reducing waste and pollution.

Environmental sustainability is also about promoting sustainable development, which is defined as economic growth that meets the needs of the present without compromising the ability of future generations to meet their own needs. This requires the integration of environmental considerations into decision-making processes and the development of sustainable practices and policies in the areas of agriculture, energy, transportation, and waste management.

Importance of Environmental Sustainability:

Environmental sustainability is critical for several reasons, including:

- Protecting the Natural World: Environmental sustainability is important for protecting the health of the planet and preserving its natural resources for future generations. This includes preserving biodiversity, protecting sensitive ecosystems, and reducing waste and pollution.

- Addressing Climate Change: Environmental sustainability is essential for addressing the pressing issue of climate change. Climate change is causing global temperatures to rise, leading to more extreme weather events, sea level rise, and the melting of polar ice caps. Addressing climate change requires reducing greenhouse gas emissions and transitioning to clean, renewable energy sources.

- Ensuring Food Security: Environmental sustainability is important for ensuring food security by protecting the health of the planet and its ecosystems. This includes promoting sustainable agriculture practices that conserve natural resources, reduce waste, and enhance the health of the soil, water, and air.

- Maintaining Economic Growth: Environmental sustainability is key to maintaining long-term economic growth and stability. A healthy environment is essential for a thriving economy, and sustainable practices in areas such as energy and resource management can lead to cost savings and economic benefits.

- Improving Human Health: Environmental sustainability is essential for improving human health. Air and water pollution, exposure to toxic chemicals, and other environmental hazards can have serious impacts on human health. By reducing these hazards and promoting sustainable practices, we can improve health outcomes and enhance quality of life for people around the world.

II: THE NATURAL ENVIRONMENT

Natural Environment:

The natural environment refers to all the living and non-living things that exist in the world around us. This includes the air we breathe, the water we drink, the land we inhabit, and the diverse array of plants, animals, and microorganisms that make up the biosphere. The natural environment is essential for life on earth and provides the resources and services that support human well-being and economic growth.

The natural environment is also a complex system that is interrelated and interconnected. For example, the health of an ecosystem, such as a forest or coral reef, depends on the health of its individual components, such as the plants, animals, and microorganisms that make up the ecosystem. This complexity is why it is important to consider the impact of our actions on the natural environment and take steps to protect and preserve the health of the planet.

One of the key challenges facing the natural environment today is climate change. Climate change is causing temperatures to rise, leading to more extreme weather events, sea level rise, and the melting of polar ice caps. Climate change also impacts ecosystems and biodiversity, as some species are unable to adapt to the changing conditions and face extinction.

Another challenge facing the natural environment is pollution, which has negative impacts on air and water quality, and the health of plants, animals, and humans. In addition, deforestation, overfishing, and soil degradation are other environmental issues that have serious impacts on the health of the planet and its ecosystems.

Earth's Ecosystems:

Ecosystems are complex systems that include all the living and non-living things in a specific area, and the relationships and interactions between them. The earth is home to a wide range of ecosystems, including forests, oceans, deserts, grasslands, and wetlands.

Each ecosystem has a unique combination of plants, animals, and microorganisms that interact with one another and with the physical environment, such as sunlight, water, and temperature. This interaction creates a delicate balance that allows the ecosystem to function and support life.

Ecosystems provide essential services and resources that support human well-being and economic growth, including food, clean water, air, and biodiversity. For example, forests provide habitat for wildlife, regulate the climate, and store carbon, while oceans provide a source of food, regulate the climate, and serve as a home for a rich diversity of life.

However, human activities, such as deforestation, overfishing, and climate change, are disrupting the delicate balance of ecosystems and causing declines in biodiversity and ecosystem health. This has serious consequences for the sustainability of the planet and the services and resources it provides.

Biodiversity and it's important:

Biodiversity refers to the variety of life on earth, including the diversity of species, ecosystems, and genes. Biodiversity is essential for the functioning of ecosystems and the provision of vital ecosystem services and resources, such as food, clean water, and air.

Biodiversity also provides aesthetic, cultural, and spiritual benefits, and contributes to human well-being. For example, protected areas and national parks offer opportunities for recreation, while the beauty of nature provides inspiration and solace.

In addition, biodiversity plays a crucial role in maintaining the balance of the earth's ecosystems and helps them to adapt to change. For example, a diverse range of species provides a buffer against the effects of climate change and helps ecosystems to recover from natural disasters and other disturbances.

However, human activities, such as deforestation, overfishing, and climate change, are causing declines in biodiversity and leading to a loss of species and habitats. This loss of biodiversity has serious consequences for the health of ecosystems, the provision of ecosystem services, and human well-being.

Climate Change:

Climate change refers to long-term changes in the average weather patterns that have come to define Earth's local and regional climates. These changes are primarily driven by increased concentrations of greenhouse gases in the atmosphere, primarily carbon dioxide, which are released by human activities such as burning fossil fuels, deforestation, and agriculture.

The consequences of climate change are far-reaching and include rising temperatures, more frequent and intense heatwaves, heavier precipitation, stronger and more frequent hurricanes, sea level rise, and melting of polar ice caps. These changes are affecting ecosystems, wildlife, and human communities, and are causing damage to infrastructure, food production, and water resources.

Climate change also exacerbates existing environmental and social problems, such as air and water pollution, disease, and conflict. In addition, it exacerbates poverty and undermines economic growth, as well as contributes to displacement and migration.

To address the challenge of climate change, it is essential to reduce greenhouse gas emissions and transition to a low-carbon economy. This requires a multi-faceted approach that includes reducing energy consumption, increasing the use of renewable energy, and promoting sustainable practices.

Air pollution:

Air pollution refers to the presence of harmful substances in the air that we breathe. These substances, known as air pollutants, include particulate matter, ozone, nitrogen oxides, sulfur dioxide, and carbon monoxide, among others.

Air pollution is caused by a variety of human activities, including the burning of fossil fuels for energy, transportation, industrial processes, and agriculture. Natural sources, such as wildfires and dust storms, also contribute to air pollution.

Air pollution has serious consequences for human health and the environment. Exposure to air pollutants can cause respiratory and cardiovascular problems and has been linked to cancer and other serious diseases. Air pollution also contributes to climate change and contributes to the acidification of the oceans.

In addition, air pollution has economic costs, as it affects tourism, reduces crop yields, and impacts the overall health of people, reducing productivity and increasing healthcare costs.

To address the challenge of air pollution, it is essential to reduce emissions of air pollutants and transition to a low-carbon economy. This requires a multi-faceted approach that includes reducing energy consumption, increasing the use of renewable energy, and promoting sustainable practices.

Water Pollution:

Water pollution refers to the presence of harmful substances in water bodies, such as lakes, rivers, oceans, and groundwater. These substances, known as water pollutants, include chemicals, pathogens, plastics, and other waste products.

Water pollution is caused by a variety of human activities, including agricultural runoff, wastewater discharge, and industrial processes. Natural sources, such as landslides and erosion, also contribute to water pollution.

Water pollution has serious consequences for human health and the environment. Exposure to water pollutants can cause illness and disease and has been linked to cancer and other serious health problems. Water pollution also affects the health of aquatic ecosystems, reducing biodiversity and damaging the food chain.

In addition, water pollution has economic costs, as it affects fishing and tourism industries, reduces crop yields, and impacts the overall health of people, reducing productivity and increasing healthcare costs.

To address the challenge of water pollution, it is essential to reduce emissions of water pollutants and promote sustainable practices. This requires a multi-faceted approach that includes reducing runoff from agriculture, improving wastewater treatment, and reducing the use of chemicals in industrial processes.

III: HUMAN IMPACT ON THE ENVIRONMENT

Human Impact on The Environment:

Human activities have a significant impact on the environment and the planet's ecosystems. The increasing population, urbanization, and consumption patterns have resulted in the depletion of natural resources and the degradation of the planet's ecosystems.

One of the primary ways that humans have impacted the environment is through the emission of greenhouse gases, which are driving climate change. The burning of fossil fuels for energy, transportation, and industrial processes is a major contributor to greenhouse gas emissions. Deforestation and land-use changes also contribute to emissions, as well as the release of methane and nitrous oxide from agriculture and waste management practices.

Another major impact that humans have on the environment is through the pollution of air, water, and soil. The release of harmful chemicals and waste products from agriculture, industrial processes, and waste management practices has contaminated water bodies and soil and has contributed to air pollution.

The human impact on the environment has also led to the loss of biodiversity and the decline of ecosystems. Habitat destruction and fragmentation, overexploitation of natural resources, and introduction of invasive species have all contributed to the loss of biodiversity and the decline of ecosystems.

To address the human impact on the environment, it is essential to adopt sustainable practices and reduce our impact on the planet. This requires a multi-faceted approach that includes reducing greenhouse gas emissions, improving waste management practices, and promoting sustainable agriculture and land-use practices.

Deforestation:

Deforestation refers to the permanent removal of forests and the conversion of forested land for other uses. It is a widespread and ongoing problem, with forests being cleared for agriculture, urbanization, and the production of wood and paper products.

Forests play a critical role in the health of the planet, providing habitat for wildlife, regulating the water cycle, and absorbing carbon dioxide from the atmosphere. Deforestation, therefore, has significant consequences for the environment and human well-being.

The loss of forests leads to the loss of biodiversity and the decline of ecosystems. Forests provide habitat for a vast array of species, and deforestation can lead to the extinction of species and the degradation of ecosystems. In addition, deforestation contributes to climate change by releasing carbon stored in the trees and soil into the atmosphere and reducing the ability of forests to absorb carbon dioxide.

Deforestation also has consequences for local communities, as forests provide livelihoods for many people, including indigenous communities, who rely on the resources and services provided by forests. Deforestation can also lead to soil erosion, degradation of water quality, and increased risk of natural disasters, such as floods and landslides.

To address the challenge of deforestation, it is essential to promote sustainable land-use practices and reduce the demand for products that contribute to deforestation, such as beef, soy, and palm oil. This requires a multi-faceted approach that includes conservation of forests, reforestation and afforestation, and sustainable agriculture and land-use practices.

Overfishing:

Overfishing is the removal of fish from the ocean at a rate faster than the rate at which they can reproduce and replenish their populations. This unsustainable fishing practice has significant consequences for the health of the oceans and the livelihoods of people who rely on fishing for their income and food security.

Overfishing leads to the decline of fish populations and the degradation of marine ecosystems. The removal of key species, such as top predators, can have cascading effects on the entire ecosystem, leading to the decline of other species and the disruption of food webs. In addition, overfishing can lead to the depletion of important habitats, such as coral reefs, which provide essential habitats for a diverse array of species.

Overfishing also has consequences for the livelihoods of people who rely on fishing for their income and food security. The decline of fish populations and the degradation of marine ecosystems can reduce the availability of fish and seafood, leading to increased competition for limited resources and reduced income for fishing communities.

To overcome the challenge of overfishing, it is essential to adopt sustainable fishing practices and reduce the demand for unsustainable seafood. This requires a multi-faceted approach that includes the implementation of fishing quotas and catch limits, the establishment of marine protected areas, and the promotion of sustainable fishing practices and the use of more selective fishing gear.

Degradation:

Land degradation refers to the decline in the quality of the land, resulting from factors such as soil erosion, nutrient depletion, salinization, and desertification. It is a widespread and ongoing problem that has significant consequences for the environment and human well-being.

Land degradation leads to the decline in the productivity of the land, reducing the ability of the land to support agriculture, forestry, and other land-based activities. The decline in productivity can also lead to reduced food security, as the land becomes less capable of producing crops and supporting livestock.

In addition, land degradation has significant consequences for the environment. Soil erosion, for example, can lead to the loss of fertile soil, reducing the ability of the land to support agriculture and other land-based activities. The decline in soil fertility can also contribute to the decline of biodiversity, as it reduces the ability of the land to support a diverse array of species.

Land degradation also has consequences for human well-being, as it can lead to increased risk of natural disasters, such as floods and landslides, and reduced access to water resources, as degraded land reduces the ability of the land to absorb and retain water.

To address the challenge of land degradation, it is essential to promote sustainable land-use practices, such as conservation tillage, cover cropping, and the use of organic matter, to improve the quality and productivity of the land. In addition, it is important to reduce the demand for products that contribute to land degradation, such as beef and soy, and promote sustainable agriculture and land-use practices.

Plastic Pollution

Plastic pollution refers to the accumulation of plastic waste in the environment, particularly in the ocean, and its impact on the ecosystem and human health. Plastic pollution is a growing problem, as the amount of plastic produced and used continues to increase, while the rate of plastic waste management and recycling remains low.

Plastic pollution has significant consequences for the environment and wildlife. Plastic waste in the ocean can entangle and harm marine animals, such as sea turtles and whales, and can also be ingested by birds and fish, leading to reduced health and reproductive success. In addition, plastic waste in the ocean can also break down into microplastics, which are small plastic particles that can be ingested by marine animals, entering the food chain, and potentially affecting human health.

Plastic pollution also has consequences for the economy and human well-being. The accumulation of plastic waste in the ocean can harm tourism and fishing industries, and the health impacts of plastic pollution, such as the potential for microplastics to enter the food chain, can have negative consequences for human health.

To address the challenge of plastic pollution, it is essential to reduce the amount of plastic produced and used and increase the rate of plastic waste management and recycling. This requires a multi-faceted approach that includes the implementation of policies and regulations, such as bans on single-use plastic items, and the promotion of sustainable alternatives, such as reusable containers and biodegradable packaging.

Energy use and its impact:

Energy use refers to the consumption of energy resources, such as oil, coal, natural gas, and renewable energy sources, to power homes, businesses, and industries. Energy use has a significant impact on the environment and human well-being, as the way we use energy can either contribute to or reduce environmental sustainability.

The use of non-renewable energy sources, such as coal, oil, and natural gas, has significant consequences for the environment. The extraction and use of these energy sources contributes to air and water pollution, as well as climate change, through the emission of greenhouse gases, such as carbon dioxide. In addition, the extraction and use of these energy sources can also result in environmental degradation, such as soil erosion, habitat destruction, and the decline of biodiversity.

On the other hand, the use of renewable energy sources, such as solar, wind, and hydro power, can reduce the impact of energy use on the environment. Renewable energy sources do not emit harmful pollutants or greenhouse gases and do not result in environmental degradation. In addition, renewable energy sources can also help to reduce the dependence on non-renewable energy sources, which are finite and will eventually become depleted.

Energy use also has a significant impact on human well-being, as it affects the cost of living, the availability of energy, and the quality of life. For example, the use of non-renewable energy sources can result in higher energy costs, as these energy sources become more expensive to extract and process, while the use of renewable energy sources can result in lower energy costs, as these energy sources are more sustainable and less expensive to produce.

To promote environmental sustainability and human well-being, it is essential to transition to a more sustainable energy system, that relies on renewable energy sources and reduces the consumption of non-renewable energy sources. This requires a multi-faceted approach that includes the implementation of policies and regulations, the promotion of energy efficiency, and the development of sustainable energy technologies.

IV: SOLUTIONS FOR ENVIRONMENTAL SUSTAINABILITY

Solutions For Environmental Sustainability:

Solving the challenges of environmental sustainability requires a multi-faceted approach that involves individuals, governments, businesses, and communities. There is no single solution to environmental sustainability, but rather a range of actions that can be taken to reduce the impact of human activities on the environment and promote sustainable development.

Individuals can play a critical role in promoting environmental sustainability by making simple changes in their daily lives, such as reducing energy use, conserving water, reducing waste, and choosing environmentally friendly products. Simple actions, such as turning off lights when leaving a room, using public transportation, or biking instead of driving, can have a significant impact on reducing the impact of human activities on the environment.

Governments can play a critical role in promoting environmental sustainability by implementing policies and regulations that encourage sustainable development, such as tax incentives for renewable energy, regulations for reducing greenhouse gas emissions, and laws for protecting natural resources and ecosystems. Governments can also invest in sustainable infrastructure, such as public transportation systems, renewable energy sources, and sustainable cities, to support a more sustainable future.

Businesses can play a critical role in promoting environmental sustainability by adopting sustainable business practices, such as reducing energy and water use, reducing waste, and using environmentally friendly products. Businesses can also invest in renewable energy sources, such as solar and wind power, to reduce their impact on the environment and to support a more sustainable future.

Communities can play a critical role in promoting environmental sustainability by coming together to promote sustainable development and to raise awareness about environmental issues. Communities can organize events, such as clean-up efforts, educational campaigns, and community gardens, to promote sustainable practices and to encourage community involvement.

Renewable Energy:

Renewable energy refers to energy sources that are replenished naturally and can be used continuously without depleting the earth's natural resources. Unlike traditional energy sources such as coal, oil, and natural gas, renewable energy sources are clean and sustainable, producing minimal or no greenhouse gas emissions and reducing the impact of human activities on the environment. Some of the most common renewable energy sources include solar, wind, hydropower, geothermal, and biomass.

Solar energy is the most abundant and accessible renewable energy source, harnessing the energy from the sun to produce electricity. Solar panels are used to capture the sun's energy and convert it into electricity for homes, businesses, and communities.

Wind energy harnesses the power of wind to generate electricity. Wind turbines are used to convert the kinetic energy of the wind into mechanical energy, which is then used to generate electricity. Wind energy is becoming increasingly popular as a source of renewable energy, as wind speeds are reliable, and the technology for harnessing wind energy has improved significantly in recent years.

Hydropower is a renewable energy source that harnesses the power of water to generate electricity. Hydroelectric dams are used to convert the kinetic energy of falling water into mechanical energy, which is then used to generate electricity. Hydropower is a clean and reliable source of renewable energy and is used extensively in many countries, particularly in areas with abundant water resources.

Geothermal energy harnesses the heat from the earth's interior to generate electricity. Geothermal power plants use the heat from hot springs, geysers, and other sources of geothermal energy to generate electricity. Geothermal energy is a clean and reliable source of renewable energy and is used extensively in many countries, particularly in areas with abundant geothermal resources.

Biomass energy is a renewable energy source that harnesses the energy stored in organic matter, such as wood, crops, and waste, to generate electricity. Biomass energy can be produced from sustainable sources, such as waste from crops or forests, or from non-sustainable sources, such as using food crops for energy production. Biomass energy can be a valuable source of renewable energy, especially in areas where other sources of renewable energy are scarce or unavailable.

Sustainable Agriculture:

Sustainable agriculture is a farming method that aims to meet the needs of present generations without compromising the ability of future generations to meet their own needs. It is a holistic approach to agriculture that considers the interrelationships between the environment, economy, and society.

Sustainable agriculture aims to minimize the negative impacts of farming on the environment while producing high-quality food and fiber in an economically and socially responsible way. This is achieved by using techniques that reduce the use of chemicals, protect soil and water resources, and conserve biodiversity.

Some of the key principles of sustainable agriculture include:

- Soil conservation: Sustainable agriculture practices aim to maintain or improve soil health by minimizing soil erosion and promoting soil fertility. This is achieved using cover crops, crop rotation, and reduced tillage practices.

- Biodiversity: Sustainable agriculture promotes biodiversity by using a diverse mix of crops and animals, which helps to maintain a healthy and balanced ecosystem. This diversity helps to reduce the risk of disease and pest outbreaks and provides habitats for beneficial insects and wildlife.

- Energy efficiency: Sustainable agriculture seeks to reduce energy use by using natural systems, such as cover crops, composting, and intercropping, to build soil fertility and reduce the need for fertilizers and pesticides.

- Water conservation: Sustainable agriculture practices aim to conserve water resources by reducing water use and improving water quality. This is achieved through practices such as crop rotation, soil conservation, and the use of drought-resistant crops.

- Economic viability: Sustainable agriculture recognizes the importance of economic viability in ensuring the long-term success of farming operations. This includes practices that improve yields, reduce costs, and increase profitability while also promoting environmental sustainability.

Conservation and Protection of Biodiversity:

Biodiversity refers to the variety of living organisms, including plants, animals, and microorganisms, and the ecosystems that support them. It is critical for the functioning of the planet's ecosystems and provides important benefits to humans, including food, medicine, and ecosystem services such as air and water purification, pollination of crops, and climate regulation.

However, human activities such as deforestation, habitat destruction, and overfishing are causing significant declines in biodiversity, threatening the stability and resilience of ecosystems and the services they provide.

Conservation and protection of biodiversity is the act of preserving, managing, and restoring the diversity of life on earth. This is achieved through a range of approaches, including:

- Protected Areas: Protected areas such as national parks, wildlife reserves, and marine protected areas are established to protect important ecosystems and their unique biodiversity.

- Species Recovery Programs: Species recovery programs aim to protect endangered species and their habitats through breeding and release programs, habitat restoration, and other conservation measures.

- Habitat Restoration: Habitat restoration involves the rehabilitation and protection of degraded or damaged habitats to support the survival and recovery of native species.

- Sustainable Harvesting: Sustainable harvesting is a conservation strategy that aims to balance the use of natural resources with their preservation. This includes the use of fishing quotas, hunting permits, and sustainable forestry practices.

- Education and Awareness: Education and awareness campaigns play an important role in promoting conservation and protection of biodiversity by raising public understanding of the value of biodiversity and the threats it faces.

Reduce, Reuse, Recycle:

Reduce, Reuse, Recycle is a widely recognized approach to waste management that aims to reduce the environmental impact of waste through reducing the amount of waste generated, reusing materials, and recycling waste materials.

- Reduce: Reducing the amount of waste generated is the most effective way to reduce the environmental impact of waste. This can be achieved by reducing consumption, choosing products with minimal packaging, and reducing the use of single-use items.

- Reuse: Reusing materials extends the life of products, reducing the need for new resources and the waste generated from production. This can be done by using reusable shopping bags, containers, and water bottles, or by repairing and refurbishing products instead of throwing them away.

- Recycle: Recycling is the process of collecting, sorting, and processing waste materials to create new products. Recycling conserves natural resources, reduces the energy needed to produce new products, and reduces greenhouse gas emissions. Common recyclable materials include paper, glass, metal, and plastic.

Implementing the Reduce, Reuse, Recycle approach helps to conserve resources, reduce greenhouse gas emissions, and mitigate the impact of waste on the environment. By adopting this approach, individuals and communities can play a vital role in creating a more sustainable future.

Sustainable Transport:

Sustainable transport refers to the use of modes of transportation that are environmentally friendly, socially responsible, and economically viable. The goal of sustainable transport is to reduce the negative impact of transportation on the environment, promote the health and well-being of communities, and support economic growth.

- Public transportation: Encouraging the use of public transportation, such as buses, trains, and subways, reduces the number of individual vehicles on the road, reducing congestion and air pollution. Public transportation also provides an alternative to car ownership, reducing the financial burden on individuals and families.

- Active transportation: Encouraging active transportation, such as cycling and walking, promotes healthy lifestyles, reduces air pollution, and reduces the number of individual vehicles on the road. This can be achieved through investment in bike lanes, sidewalks, and pedestrian crossings.

- Electric vehicles: Encouraging the use of electric vehicles reduces greenhouse gas emissions, as electric vehicles produce fewer emissions than gasoline-powered vehicles. This can be achieved through investment in charging infrastructure, offering financial incentives for electric vehicle purchase, and promoting the use of electric vehicles in fleets.

- Improved logistics and delivery: Improving logistics and delivery systems can reduce the environmental impact of transportation. For example, optimizing delivery routes and using fuel-efficient vehicles can reduce emissions and energy use.

V: GOVERNMENT AND BUSINESS ACTION FOR SUSTAINABILITY

Government and Business Action for Sustainability:

Government and business action is crucial for achieving environmental sustainability. Both government and business have a critical role to play in creating policies, investing in sustainable technologies, and educating the public about the importance of sustainability.

- Government Action: Governments can play a critical role in promoting environmental sustainability by creating policies and regulations that encourage sustainable practices. This can include creating incentives for renewable energy development, promoting public transportation, and implementing regulations that limit pollution. Governments can also provide funding for research and development of sustainable technologies and educate the public about the importance of sustainability.

- Business Action: Businesses can play a critical role in promoting environmental sustainability by investing in sustainable technologies, implementing sustainable practices, and promoting sustainable products and services. This can include investing in renewable energy, reducing waste, and promoting environmentally friendly products and services. Businesses can also play a role in educating the public about the importance of sustainability and encouraging sustainable practices among their employees and customers.

Environmental Regulations:

Environmental regulations are laws and regulations that are designed to protect the environment and human health. They are implemented by government agencies, such as the Environmental Protection Agency (EPA), to control and reduce pollution, protect natural resources, and promote sustainability.

- Emission Standards: Emission standards are regulations that limit the amount of pollutants that can be released into the air, water, and land. This can include emissions from industrial processes, transportation, and energy production. Emission standards play a critical role in reducing air and water pollution, protecting public health, and promoting sustainability.

- Resource Management Regulations: Resource management regulations are designed to protect natural resources, such as forests, water resources, and wildlife. These regulations can include restrictions on the use of certain chemicals, limits on the amount of water that can be withdrawn from a river, and restrictions on the use of natural resources in certain areas.

- Product Standards: Product standards are regulations that set standards for the production and use of products that have a significant impact on the environment. This can include standards for products such as energy-efficient appliances, electric vehicles, and building materials. These standards play a critical role in reducing energy use, promoting sustainability, and protecting the environment.

- Waste Management Regulations: Waste management regulations are designed to reduce the amount of waste that is generated, promote recycling, and protect public health and the environment. This can include regulations on the disposal of hazardous waste, restrictions on the use of certain chemicals, and requirements for proper recycling and waste management practices.

Corporate Social Responsibility:

Corporate Social Responsibility (CSR) is a concept that refers to the responsibility of corporations to act in an ethical and sustainable manner, and to consider the impact of their operations on society, the environment, and stakeholders. CSR is often seen as a way for companies to go beyond their legal obligations and to create a positive impact in the communities in which they operate.

Environmental Protection: CSR often involves a commitment to environmental protection, including reducing the company's carbon footprint, reducing waste, and promoting sustainable practices. Companies can implement CSR by investing in renewable energy, reducing emissions, and promoting sustainability throughout their operations.

Social Responsibility: CSR also involves a commitment to social responsibility, including improving working conditions, promoting equality and diversity, and providing education and training opportunities to employees. Companies can implement CSR by promoting fair and ethical labor practices, supporting community development, and providing opportunities for employee growth and development.

Stakeholder Engagement: CSR also involves engaging with stakeholders, including employees, customers, suppliers, and communities. Companies can implement CSR by promoting transparency, consultation, and collaboration with stakeholders, and by considering the impact of their operations on stakeholders.

Reporting and Transparency: Companies that engage in CSR are often expected to be transparent about their practices and to report on their progress. This can include publishing sustainability reports, conducting regular audits, and engaging in stakeholder engagement initiatives.

Public-Private Partnerships:

Public-Private Partnerships (PPPs) refer to collaborations between government and private sector organizations to achieve common goals. In the context of environmental sustainability, PPPs can be used to address a range of environmental challenges, such as climate change, environmental degradation, and resource depletion.

Benefits of PPPs: PPPs can provide a range of benefits, including increased investment, access to expertise and technology, and improved efficiency. For example, a PPP between a government and a private sector company might lead to the development of new renewable energy technologies, or the creation of new protected areas to conserve biodiversity.

Roles and Responsibilities: In a PPP, each partner has specific roles and responsibilities, and the partnership is governed by a set of agreed upon rules and regulations. Governments may provide funding, regulate activities, and enforce environmental standards, while private sector partners may provide expertise, technology, and investment.

Transparency and Accountability: PPPs must be transparent and accountable, with clear reporting mechanisms and independent evaluations of the partnership's performance. This helps to ensure that the partnership is aligned with the goals of both partners and that the partnership is delivering the intended benefits.

Challenges: Despite the potential benefits of PPPs, there are also challenges that must be addressed. For example, PPPs can be complex and time-consuming to set up and manage, and there may be concerns about the balance of power between government and private sector partners. In addition, there may be conflicts between the interests of different partners, which must be managed to ensure the success of the partnership.

The Role of the Consumer in Driving Change:

The role of consumers in driving change towards environmental sustainability is increasingly important as consumer demand and choices can influence the behavior of businesses and governments. Here are some key points to consider in the role of consumers in driving change:

- Awareness and Education: Consumers play a crucial role in promoting environmental sustainability by becoming informed and educated about environmental issues and making informed choices about their consumption patterns. This includes understanding the environmental impact of different products and services and seeking out environmentally friendly alternatives.

- Consumer Demand: Consumers have the power to drive change by demanding environmentally friendly products and services. When consumers demand environmentally friendly products, businesses respond by offering them, which can lead to a shift in production and consumption patterns. This can also drive innovation and investment in sustainable products and technologies.

- Vote with your Wallet: Consumers can also vote with their wallets by choosing to support companies and products that have a positive impact on the environment. This sends a clear signal to companies and governments that there is demand for sustainable products and practices.

- Lifestyle Changes: Consumers can make a difference by making changes to their own lifestyles. This includes reducing energy use, waste reduction, and adopting sustainable transportation options.

- Community Action: Consumers can also get involved in community initiatives that promote environmental sustainability, such as volunteering for local environmental organizations or participating in local sustainability initiatives.

VI: THE FUTURE OF ENVIRONMENTAL SUSTAINABILITY

The Future of Environmental Sustainability:

The future of environmental sustainability is uncertain, but it will largely depend on the actions taken by individuals, governments, and businesses in the coming years. Here are some key factors that will shape the future of environmental sustainability:

- Technological Advancements: Technological advancements have the potential to significantly impact environmental sustainability. New technologies, such as renewable energy sources and sustainable agriculture practices, can help to reduce the negative impact of human activities on the environment.

- Government Policy: Government policies and regulations play a critical role in promoting environmental sustainability. Governments can implement policies that encourage the development of sustainable technologies and practices and enforce regulations that limit the negative impact of human activities on the environment.

- Business Action: The role of businesses in promoting environmental sustainability will also be important. Companies that adopt sustainable practices and invest in environmentally friendly technologies can help to drive change and promote sustainability.

- Consumer Behavior: Consumers play a critical role in promoting environmental sustainability by making informed choices about their consumption patterns. Consumers can demand environmentally friendly products and services, and support companies that have a positive impact on the environment.

- Climate Change: Climate change will continue to be a major challenge in the future of environmental sustainability. The world will need to take significant action to reduce greenhouse gas emissions and address the impacts of climate change to ensure a sustainable future.

Emerging Technologies and Innovations:

Emerging technologies and innovations have the potential to play a significant role in promoting environmental sustainability. Here are some examples of emerging technologies and innovations that could impact environmental sustainability:

- Renewable Energy Technologies: Advances in renewable energy technologies, such as wind and solar power, have the potential to greatly reduce our dependence on fossil fuels and reduce greenhouse gas emissions.

- Electric Vehicles: The increasing popularity of electric vehicles is a promising development for environmental sustainability. Electric vehicles are much more environmentally friendly than traditional gasoline-powered vehicles and can greatly reduce greenhouse gas emissions and air pollution.

- Sustainable Agriculture: Innovations in sustainable agriculture can help to reduce the negative impact of food production on the environment. New technologies, such as precision agriculture and vertical farming, can help to reduce water use and increase food production while minimizing the impact on the environment.

- Waste Management: New technologies and innovations in waste management, such as recycling and composting, can help to reduce the amount of waste that is produced and reduce the negative impact of waste on the environment.

- Green Building: Innovations in green building technology, such as sustainable materials and energy-efficient design, can help to reduce the energy use of buildings and reduce greenhouse gas emissions.

- Smart Grid Technologies: Smart grid technologies, such as advanced metering infrastructure and demand response programs, can help to reduce energy use and increase the efficiency of energy distribution.

These are just a few examples of the many emerging technologies and innovations that have the potential to impact environmental sustainability. As technology continues to advance, it is likely that new and innovative solutions to environmental challenges will emerge, helping to create a more sustainable future for all.

Global Cooperation for Sustainability:

Global cooperation is critical for addressing environmental sustainability challenges and promoting sustainable practices across the world. Here are some ways that global cooperation can contribute to environmental sustainability:

- Climate Change: Climate change is a global issue that requires collective action. International agreements, such as the Paris Agreement, provide a framework for countries to work together to reduce greenhouse gas emissions and tackle the impacts of climate change.

- Biodiversity Conservation: Biodiversity is threatened on a global scale, and international cooperation is necessary to protect endangered species and their habitats. For example, the Convention on Biological Diversity is an international treaty aimed at conserving biological diversity and promoting sustainable use of its components.

- Sustainable Resource Management: Natural resources, such as forests, oceans, and freshwater systems, are often managed on a global scale. International cooperation can help to ensure that these resources are used in a sustainable manner and conserve their value for future generations.

- Trade and Investment: The global trade and investment system has a significant impact on environmental sustainability. International cooperation can help to ensure that trade and investment practices are environmentally responsible and promote sustainable development.

- Capacity Building: Many countries, particularly those in the developing world, lack the capacity to tackle environmental sustainability challenges on their own. International cooperation can help to build capacity and provide technical assistance to support sustainable development.

- Science and Technology: Science and technology play a crucial role in addressing environmental sustainability challenges. International cooperation can help to promote scientific research and development of new technologies, as well as facilitate the transfer of knowledge and technology to countries that need it most.

Global cooperation is essential for addressing environmental sustainability challenges and promoting sustainable practices across the world. By working together, countries can share resources, knowledge, and expertise to create a more sustainable future for all.

The Importance of Education and Awareness:

Education and awareness are crucial components of promoting environmental sustainability. Here are some ways that education and awareness can contribute to environmental sustainability:

Understanding the Issues: Environmental sustainability encompasses a wide range of complex issues, such as climate change, biodiversity loss, and pollution. Education and awareness can help individuals understand these issues and the impact that their actions can have on the environment.

Promoting Sustainable Behaviors: By providing individuals with the knowledge and skills needed to make environmentally responsible decisions, education and awareness can help to promote sustainable behaviors, such as reducing waste, conserving energy, and protecting biodiversity.

Raising Awareness: Environmental sustainability challenges can be difficult to understand and often receive limited media attention. Education and awareness initiatives can help to raise awareness about these challenges and engage individuals in the conservation of the environment.

Encouraging Action: Education and awareness can help to motivate individuals to take action on environmental sustainability challenges. By providing individuals with the information and tools they need to make a difference, education and awareness can inspire them to become agents of change.

Building a Culture of Sustainability: Education and awareness can help to create a culture of environmental sustainability. By educating individuals about the importance of sustainable practices and encouraging them to incorporate these practices into their daily lives, education and awareness can help to build a foundation for a more sustainable future.

Education and awareness are essential components of promoting environmental sustainability. By providing individuals with the knowledge and skills they need to make environmentally responsible decisions, education and awareness can help to create a more sustainable future for all.

Personal Action for a Sustainable Future:

Personal action is a critical component of creating a sustainable future. Here are some ways that individuals can take action towards environmental sustainability:

Reduce Energy Usage: One of the easiest ways to reduce your carbon footprint is to conserve energy. This can be done by turning off lights and electronics when not in use, using energy-efficient appliances, and using public transportation or carpooling instead of driving alone.

Reduce Waste: Reducing waste is another important aspect of environmental sustainability. This can be done by recycling, composting, and reducing the use of single-use plastics.

Support Sustainable Products: When making purchasing decisions, individuals can support companies and products that are environmentally friendly and sustainable. This includes choosing products that are made from environmentally friendly materials and produced through sustainable manufacturing processes.

Support Sustainable Agriculture: Supporting sustainable agriculture can help to reduce the impact of agriculture on the environment. This includes choosing products grown through sustainable farming practices, such as organic farming, and reducing the consumption of meat, which can have a significant impact on the environment.

Get Involved: Individuals can also get involved in environmental sustainability initiatives, such as participating in beach cleanups, supporting environmental organizations, and advocating for environmentally friendly policies.

Educate Others: Education and awareness play a critical role in promoting environmental sustainability. By sharing information about environmental sustainability with friends and family, individuals can help to spread the word and create a more sustainable future for all.

Personal action is key to creating a sustainable future. By making environmentally responsible choices and getting involved in initiatives that promote environmental sustainability, individuals can make a positive impact on the environment and help to create a more sustainable future for all.

VII. CONCLUSION

Summary of Key Points:

The Summary of Key Points section in a book on Environmental Sustainability should highlight the most important concepts and ideas discussed throughout the book. This section should be a brief, yet comprehensive, overview of the book's content.

Some key points to include in the Summary of Key Points section might include:

- Definition of Environmental Sustainability: Environmental sustainability is the ability to meet the needs of the present without compromising the ability of future generations to meet their own needs.

- Importance of Environmental Sustainability: Environmental sustainability is critical for the survival of our planet and future generations. The natural environment is under threat from human activities, such as deforestation, overfishing, and plastic pollution, as well as the impacts of climate change and air and water pollution.

- Overview of Earth's Ecosystems: Earth's ecosystems, including forests, oceans, and grasslands, provide essential services and support life on the planet. Biodiversity is also important, as it ensures the resilience of the earth's ecosystems and the survival of species.

- Climate Change: Climate change is a major environmental issue that is caused by the release of greenhouse gases, such as carbon dioxide, into the atmosphere. This is leading to rising temperatures and sea levels, which are having a profound impact on the earth's ecosystems and wildlife.

- Human Impact on the Environment: Human activities, such as deforestation, overfishing, and plastic pollution, are having a significant impact on the natural environment. The use of energy, such as coal and oil, is also contributing to air and water pollution and the release of greenhouse gases.

- Solutions for Environmental Sustainability: There are many solutions for environmental sustainability, including renewable energy, sustainable agriculture, conservation, and protection of biodiversity, reduce, reuse, and recycle, sustainable transport, and public-private partnerships. Emerging technologies and innovations, along with global cooperation, will also play a critical role in creating a sustainable future.

- Government and Business Action for Sustainability: Governments and businesses play a critical role in creating a sustainable future. Environmental regulations, corporate social responsibility, and public-private partnerships can help to drive change and create a more sustainable future.

- Personal Action for a Sustainable Future: Individuals can also play a role in creating a more sustainable future. This includes educating others and taking personal action, such as reducing waste, using energy-efficient products, and supporting sustainable products and companies.

The Importance of Continued Action for Sustainability:

The continued action for environmental sustainability is crucial for ensuring a healthy and livable planet for future generations. The environmental challenges faced by the world today require collective and sustained effort from all sectors of society. The rapid pace of development and population growth has resulted in the degradation of natural resources, which has had far-reaching impacts on the environment. If we are to overcome these challenges, it is essential that individuals, governments, and businesses all work together to promote sustainable practices.

Continued action for sustainability is needed to address ongoing environmental issues, such as climate change, deforestation, water and air pollution, and the loss of biodiversity. These issues pose a threat to the health of both the planet and its inhabitants, and must be addressed through a combination of technology, innovation, education, and collective action.

In addition, continued action is needed to ensure that the progress that has been made towards sustainability is not reversed. Governments, businesses, and individuals must continue to work together to promote sustainable practices and protect the environment. This requires continued investment in renewable energy, sustainable agriculture, conservation and protection of biodiversity, and efforts to reduce waste and promote recycling.

Education and awareness also play a critical role in ensuring the continued action for sustainability. It is essential that individuals understand the impact of their actions on the environment and the importance of sustainable practices. Governments, businesses, and organizations must also continue to educate the public on the importance of sustainability and the steps that can be taken to protect the environment.

Conclusion:

The conclusion of a book on Environmental Sustainability should summarize the key points made throughout the book and emphasize the importance of addressing environmental sustainability as a global issue.

Environmental sustainability is critical for the survival of our planet and future generations. The natural environment, including the earth's ecosystems and biodiversity, is under threat from human activities such as deforestation, overfishing, and plastic pollution, as well as the impacts of climate change and air and water pollution. Governments, businesses, and consumers all have a role to play in creating a more sustainable future.

Solutions for environmental sustainability include renewable energy, sustainable agriculture, conservation, and protection of biodiversity, reduce, reuse, and recycle, sustainable transport, and public-private partnerships. Emerging technologies and innovations, along with global cooperation, will also play a critical role in creating a sustainable future.

Education and awareness are also essential components of environmental sustainability. By educating others and taking personal action, individuals can help to drive change and create a more sustainable future.

In conclusion, environmental sustainability is a complex and pressing issue that requires immediate action. By working together and taking personal responsibility, we can create a sustainable future that protects the natural environment and ensures the survival of our planet and future generations.

Final Thoughts and Recommendations:

The final thoughts and recommendations section of a book on environmental sustainability is a crucial part that ties everything together and emphasizes the importance of continued action. This section should summarize the key takeaways from the book and provide concrete recommendations for individuals, organizations, and governments.

Firstly, the importance of continued action should be highlighted. Environmental sustainability is a complex and ongoing challenge that requires the commitment and effort of everyone, from individuals to governments. The solutions discussed in the book, such as renewable energy, sustainable agriculture, conservation, and protection of biodiversity, and reducing, reusing, and recycling, are just the start. They must be sustained and improved upon to make a meaningful impact on the environment.

Secondly, the role of education and awareness should be emphasized. Education is crucial in creating a sustainable future, as it empowers individuals to make informed decisions and to act in an environmentally responsible manner. In addition, it is important to raise public awareness of environmental issues, such as climate change and pollution, so that people understand the impact of their actions and the urgency of the situation.

Finally, the need for global cooperation and collaboration should be emphasized. Environmental sustainability is a global issue, and it requires a coordinated effort from all nations to tackle it effectively. Countries must work together to reduce emissions, protect biodiversity, and promote sustainable practices, such as renewable energy and sustainable agriculture. Only through collaboration can the world achieve environmental sustainability and secure a healthy future for generations to come.

In conclusion, the final thoughts and recommendations section of the book should emphasize the continued importance of action, the role of education and awareness, and the need for global cooperation and collaboration. The book should encourage readers to take personal responsibility for the environment and to act in an environmentally responsible manner, and provide concrete recommendations for governments, organizations, and individuals to take action towards a more sustainable future.